Usborne
Sticker Dolly Dressing
Around the World

Illustrated by Jo Moore

Written by Emily Bone and designed by Stella Baggott

Contents

Folk festival (Austria)

In a sunny Austrian town, three friends are on their way to a summer folk festival. Sabine and Birgit are dressed in bright red skirts made from wool, with fresh flowers tucked into their bodices. Kristof is wearing leather shorts, called lederhosen.

Sabine

Birgit

Kristof

Bride and groom (Japan)

In a tranquil water garden, a Japanese bride and groom are about to be married. They are both dressed in striking silk robes, called kimonos, that have long, wide sleeves. The bride's kimono is red and white, to bring good luck. The groom wears a striped skirt, or hakama, over his kimono.

Kumiko

Toru

Reindeer herders (Norway)

Inga, Tilda and Morten spend hours in the freezing snow herding reindeer. Their clothes are made from dyed animal skins, fur and wool to keep them warm. The bright patterns around their collars and cuffs show which village they come from.

Inga

Tilda

Morten

Carnival time (Mexico)

A carnival has arrived in town, and three friends can't wait to join in the celebrations. Catalina and Salma have braided red, green and white ribbons into their hair. They're wearing bright, sparkly skirts. Cesar's costume is called a charro or cowboy suit, because Mexican cowboys used to dress in a similar way.

Catalina

Salma

Cesar

Indian wedding

At a lavish Indian wedding, the happy bride and groom stand on a stage while their guests bring them gifts, such as delicious sweets. The bride and her sister wear beautiful silk saris and their hands and feet are patterned with dye that will fade over time. The groom is dressed in a long silk jacket, called a sherwani.

Brinda

Shireen

Ravi

A family dinner (Korea)

Soo Min is having dinner at her grandparents' house dressed in a traditional Korean outift, called a hanbok. Her long skirt and jacket are made from stiff silk, and as she walks they sound like rustling leaves.

Soo Min

Cambodian dancer

In an ancient palace, Jorani is performing a traditional dance. She wears a shining golden crown, and her wrists are covered in glittering, jewel-studded bracelets.

Jorani

Village life (Nigeria)

A Nigerian couple and their friend are walking home from church in the scorching midday heat. They are wearing light cotton clothes to keep them cool, and both women protect their heads with brightly patterned headscarves, called geles. The man is dressed in a loose-fitting shirt, known as a buba.

Ebun

Sade

Obi

Flamenco dancers (Spain)

In a town square in southern Spain, two women are about to perform a lively dance, called the flamenco. Luisa is wearing an elegant dress, decorated with lots of lacy ruffles, while Ana is holding castanets that she will play during the dance. Pablo will accompany the dancers on his guitar.

Pablo

Ana

Luisa

In the mountains (Tibet)

These Tibetan farmers are wearing their finest clothes because they're at a festival celebrating the new harvest. As it's so high up in the mountains, they keep warm in thick silk robes, lined with fur. They're also wearing chunky necklaces and belts made from gold, silver and valuable gemstones.

Pema

Sonam

Jangmu

At the dance (Poland)

Petra, Tomas and Magda are Polish folk dancers, getting ready to perform a quick dance called the polka. Petra and Magda are wearing bright red necklaces made from coral, and pretty flower garlands in their hair. Tomas has feathers in his hat.

Tomas

Petra

Tomas

Magda

A mountain village (Peru)

Luis, Pilar and Carmen are returning to their village in the mountains, after a day tending their llama herd. The women are wearing bright jackets made from wool and decorated with lots of buttons. Luis's handwoven shawl, called a poncho, keeps him warm.

Luis

Pilar

Carmen

World map

On this page, you can find out where in the world the costumes in this book come from. Stick each costume in the correct place on the map.

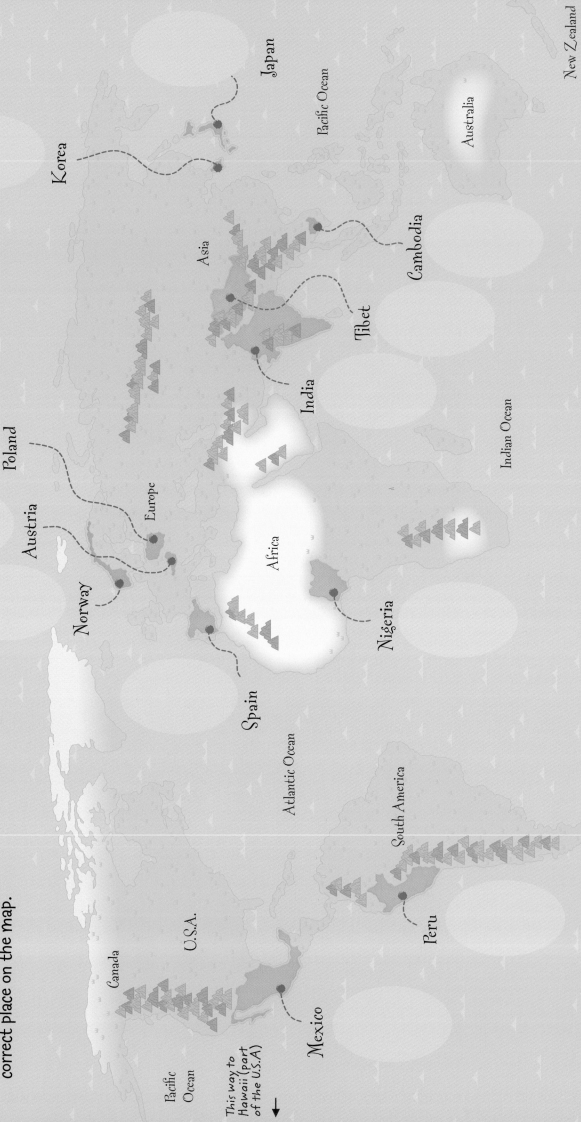

Canada

U.S.A.

Pacific Ocean

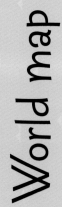
This way to Hawaii (part of the U.S.A)

Mexico

Atlantic Ocean

South America

Peru

Spain

Norway

Austria

Poland

Europe

Africa

Nigeria

Asia

India

Tibet

Cambodia

Korea

Japan

Pacific Ocean

Indian Ocean

Australia

New Zealand

This way to Antarctica